# Raspberry Pi 3

## An Ultimate Walkthrough to The Raspberry Pi 3

# Contents

# Introduction

I want to thank you and congratulate you for purchasing this book "Raspberry Pi 3: An Ultimate Walkthrough to the Raspberry Pi 3".

This book will give you a good grounding in getting started with your new Raspberry Pi 3, the tiny budget computer that does more than you could ever believe. We'll talk about the specs of this credit-card sized computer, how to set it up and how to code it using Python. If you are not au fait with Python, don't worry because I will give you an overview of the basics, everything you need to know. Lastly, I'll give you a couple of projects to get started with and a few tips on using your Raspberry Pi 3.

Raspberry Pi 3 came out in February 2016 and, tiny and barebones as it is, it is thrashing the competition into oblivion. If you love to tinker, love to build your own devices and love to get your hands dirty with a bit of coding then Raspberry Pi 3 is for you. It's cheap, it's cheerful and, with a bit of practice, dead simple to use.

I expect you to be a newbie to the Raspberry Pi so I have gone back to basics with all the instructions you need to learn how to use your neat little computer. I'll also be giving you the commands you need to get around Raspbian, the Linux-based operating system on your Raspberry Pi 3.

Are you ready to learn how to be an expert at the Raspberry Pi 3? Are you ready to start learning just what this amazing little computer can do? Then delve in and let's get going!

# Chapter 1

# An Overview of the Raspberry Pi 3

The Raspberry Pi was originally released as a way of providing a cheaper alternative to the expensive gaming consoles and computers that were flooding the market. It was designed to teach children the joys of computer programming, a way to make their own device on a budget. If your budget really is a shoestring, then the Raspberry Pi 3 may just be the answer you have been looking for.

The Raspberry Pi 3 is the latest model of the popular credit-card sized computer, released in February of 2016. It costs just $35 for the basic Raspberry Pi 3 but what you get for your money is quite astounding. With specs that match some of the computers on the market today, you won't get better for such a small price tag.

## What has the Raspberry Pi 3 Got?

Raspberry Pi 3 is nothing more than a circuit board but there are plenty of peripherals that you can buy to make that circuit board into whatever you want. So, what is on this little board? For a start, you can expect a couple of USB ports, an HDMI port so can connect a monitor and a slot for an SD card as well as an Ethernet connector. Take a look at that and you can already see that you have the basics needed to create a computer CPU. What you do with it will depend entirely on what you install on it and how good you are at coding if you want to achieve more than just what can be downloaded online.

When you first start out with your Raspberry Pi, you are going to need an SD card. Try to go for at least a 4GB card at Class 4 speed because this is where your operating system and applications are going to be stored. Raspbian OS, the operating system for the Pi will be stored here and you can download that from the official Raspberry Pi website. If you want to store other applications, software or programming codes, go for a minimum 8 GB to be safe.

**Raspberry Pi 3 Specs**

Let's look at what you get for your money:

- **Size -** 3.5 inches by 2.5 inches
- **Connectivity -** Bluetooth 4.1 and 802.11n Wi-Fi
- **Ram** – 1 GB SDRAM
- **CPU** – quad-core, 1.2 GHz – 64-bit Broadcom ARM 48 processors
- **Audio output -** headphone or HDMI
- **Video output** – composite or HDMI
- **GPU** – 4000 MHz VideoCore IV
- **Ethernet** – 10/100
- **USB ports** – 4
- **Ethernet port**
- Display interface
- Micro SD slot
- 3.5mm composite slot for headphones and video
- Camera interface

## Hardware

At its very basic, Raspberry Pi 3 is a miniature computer and that means you will find many of the components that are on a typical laptop or desktop computer. Let's look a bit closer at the hardware:

## System-on-Chip (SoC)

The SoC chip is manufactured by Broadcom and the Raspberry Pi 3 is the only model of the Pi that contains this chip – it is the chip that is used in the first generation of smartphones

## CPU

The central processing unit of the Raspberry Pi 3 has an ARM quad-core processor cortex A35. In a basic laptop or desktop, you will find the cortex A15 so you can see how much more powerful the Raspberry Pi 3 is. The 1.2 GHz chip has twin cores that are backed up by a 1 GB LPDDR2 module and run at 32 KB level 1 and 512 KB level 2 cache.

## GPU

The graphic processing unit is capable of 25 FLOPS and can be used for viewing MPEG 2 and VC1 as well as 1080p pictures and videos. To give you a better idea, the graphics are said to be as good as those in the Xbox 360.

## Memory

The Micro SD slot is found on the flip side of the circuit board and is used as detectable memory. You normally use these to store external applications, software, documents and files that are necessary for the GPU and CPU to use.

## RAM

The random-access memory is 1 GB, using 512 MB or less with the GPU. That enables faster 1080p rendering and advanced 3D video playing. The rest of the RAM is used by the CPU.

## Ports

The Raspberry Pi 3 has an Ethernet port that is used to connect the board physically to the internet. The

USB ports, of which there are 2, are used for peripherals, like a mouse or a keyboard and there is a mini-USB jack for the power. There are also audio and video out ports.

## CSI

The camera serial interface provides the bandwidth that the processor needs to talk to a camera that has been attached to RPi 2 board

## DSI

The display serial interface allows you to connect a monitor, television, or computer, including touch screen monitors.

## Wi-Fi

As well as the Ethernet port, Raspberry Pi 3 also has built-in Wi-Fi at 802.11n support to allow wireless internet connection. It is worth noting that this is the first Pi model that has been able to do this.

## Bluetooth

Raspberry Pi 3 has built-in Bluetooth 4.1 and, again, this is the first model with this feature

If you have an earlier model of the Raspberry Pi it is worth considering the upgrade to the Raspberry Pi 3, if only for the fact that you get Bluetooth and Wi-Fi. This expands its versatility, whatever you use it for, you can use it anywhere.

# Chapter 2

# The Desktop and Connecting the Raspberry Pi 3

Before you can connect your Pi3 to the desktop you need to have these peripherals:

**1. Input Device**

This would be a keyboard and a mouse, either Bluetooth or USB. Do be aware that, as Raspberry Pi has limited power, it has the potential to be somewhat unpredictable if a mouse or a keyboard takes too much power so stick to simple basic models. Don't go for a keyboard that has loads of flashing lights and a ton of features – you won't need them with the Pi

**2. Video Cable – HDMI**

This is the best way to connect a TV or monitor to your Pi as it already has a full HDMI port. If you use an older TV or a VGA monitor, you would be better off getting a converter as it will work better

## 3. USB Power Supply

You can use a micro USB power supply for this but make sure it is a 2500m/A or 5.1V-2.5A as this will give you the best performance. If you have the Pi 2, you can use the 5V-2A power supply it runs on but you may get some performance issues. Alternatively, purchase a Pi power bank – this can be attached to the USB or the GP10 pins.

## 4. Audio Jack

This is for the sound if you are not intending to use the HDMI and it should be 3.5mm. This is helpful if you wanted to add another speaker that already has a 3.5mm jack and didn't want to use the HDMI.

## 5. TV or Monitor

Raspberry PI 3 has an HD video feed of 1080p and the HDMI port. You can use a monitor or TV that connects through HDMI or, if that isn't an option for you, you will need to purchase an HDMI to DVI converter to attach your monitor. If your monitor is VGA, you will need to make sure that the HDMI to VGA converter is compatible with Raspberry Pi 3. LED TVs can be connected with the HDMI and older televisions will require an RCA connection – you won't get such good pictures this way though

## 6. MicroSD Card

Raspberry Pi 3 has that all-important SD card slot and this is going to be the storage place for the Raspbian operating system and some software and applications. As a minimum, you really need to consider an 8 GB card but higher is better obviously – the bigger the storage, the more you can get on it! You can purchase MicroSD cards that are specific to the Pi and already contain the operating system or you can just buy a normal SD card and download the operating system onto it from the Raspberry Pi website.

## 7. MicroSD Card Writer

Check that your computer has a card reader/writer. If not, you will need to buy one. The Raspberry Pi 3 does NOT have a built-in writer and if your MicroSD is going to be your primary media for file transfers over to your PC then you need a card writer.

## 8. USB Thumb Drives

Sometimes known as USB keys, these are useful for the transfer of small files between computers. If you don't want to have a larger drive attached or you want your Raspberry Pi 3 to be mobile, USB keys are the way to go

## 9. External Hard Drive

If you intend to use your RASPBERRY PI 3 on a continuous basis, consider investing in an external hard drive – 500 GB or 1 TB. However, do keep in mind that they do use a lot of power and, if you are powering your Raspberry Pi 3 via a power bank, you should expect to experience some performance issues

## 10. Camera Module

You can use a camera module with Raspberry Pi 3 provided it is compatible – you can get Raspberry Pi 3 compatible ones online. Raspberry Pi 3 sill supports a module up to 5 megapixels and can be used for shooting HD video or photos

## 11. Pi Case

This isn't necessarily classed as a peripheral but you should keep your Raspberry Pi 3 chipset in a case to keep it protected from damage, both while in use or in storage. Make sure you get the right case for your model! If you are lucky enough to have a 3D printer, you could even design and make your own.

In the next chapter, we are going to take a look at the Raspbian OS.

# Chapter 3

# Setting Up Raspbian

We are going to look at how to download and install Raspbian from your computer and how to get it all set up ready for use:

**Install Raspbian**

Raspbian is the most popular operating system for both beginner and for experienced Pi users, simply because of the desktop GUI. What that means is you don't need to type in reams of code to pull files up, run programs or check directories. With the desktop graphical user interface, you can access pretty much everything that you need to with a mouse and navigate it in the same way as you do your current mobile or desktop OS.

Here's how to install Raspbian OS.

## 1. Download Raspbian

On your computer browser go to www.raspberrypi.org/downloads and download the latest version. It should be around 500MB, a good deal bigger than many other distributions and this is because it is a fully featured distribution with a great user interface.

## 2. Load RPI Installer

You will need the Win32diskimager installer and for that, you need to go to http://sourceforge.net/projects/win32diskimager/. What this does is allows you to copy the image for Raspbian that you downloaded in the first step straight to your MicroSD card. Once you have the installer, unzip the Raspbian zip file.

## 3. Choose Your Image File

Open the Win 32 Disk Imager and pick the image file that is to be copied over to the MicroSD card. Click the folder icon that is above the option for Image File. Next, click the image you want to use and click OK

## 4. Choose your MicroSD card

Go to Device menu and choose the card that you are copying the OS to. Ensure that the card has already been formatted as FAT32 as this is the format recognized by Raspberry Pi 3. Be aware that, once the card has been selected, any data that is already on the card will be wiped off so, if you are happy that you have the right card, click Write

## 5. Wait for Writing to Complete

The image writing process will begin and the file you chose will be copied over to the SD card - how long it takes depends on the speed of your SD card but, typically, it will take a few minutes. If you are struggling to write to the card, start again but run Win 32 Disk Imager as administrator instead by right-clicking the icon and choosing **Run as Administrator**

## 6. Boot Up the OS

When the Write process has completed, eject the card safely from your computer and put it into your Raspberry Pi 3. When you switch on the Pi3, you will see a setup menu. The default values are already there so just press Enter until you get to the Command Prompt. At the prompt, type in **startx** and then hit Enter again. This will load up the Raspbian GUI.

## Using Raspbian for the First Time

When your RASPBERRY PI 3 is powered up for the first time and Raspbian has been loaded, you will automatically be taken to the Raspberry Pi 3 Software Configuration Tool, otherwise known as Raspi-config. This shows you a menu where you can change some of the Raspberry Pi 3 settings. Take note, while you are doing this, you can't use your mouse, at least not yet. To navigate through each option, use the arrow keys on your keyboard or use the Tab key. Press Enter to confirm each choice – there will be a short delay between pressing Enter and the next menu appearing.

Once you are in Raspi-config, you will see the following options:

## 1. Expand Filesystem

If you installed Raspbian from a pre-installed card, then you can ignore this option as you will have all the space on your card to use. If, however, you used the image option as detailed above, you will need to make sure this option is selected to optimize your SD card when your Raspberry Pi 3 is launched for the very first time.

## 2. Change User Password

For security purposes, you should change the default user password – the user is set as "pi". Select the option and type your new password at the bottom of the screen and then type it again to confirm.

## 3. Enable Boot to Desktop/Scratch

Normally, when you power up your Raspberry Pi 3, it will automatically go to the Linux command prompt and this is where you type in your commands. If you choose this option, you will go straight to the graphical user interface desktop.

## 4. Internationalization Options: Change Locale

You can change the language setting here but, if you are happy with English, ignore this option

## 5. Internationalization Options: Change Time zone

Raspberry Pi 3 can detect your time zone automatically when you connect to the internet but you do need to select this option now to ensure that the time and date settings are correct. You can choose your region and the city closest to your time zone

## 6. Internationalization Options: Change Keyboard Layout

When you select this option, you see the name and model of a number of different keyboards. This is where you set yours up to make sure you get the best use out of it. If you don't see yours on the list, choose a generic setting so that you can use the symbols that you are used to seeing on your normal OS.

You can also set up Compose key here; this lets you input characters that aren't normally present on the keyboard. You can also enable the option of **Ctrl+Alt+Backspace** so that you close X Server quickly.

### 7. Enable Camera

Choosing this option lets you toggle the camera off and on if one is attached to the Raspberry Pi 3

### 8. Add to Rastrack

Rastrack is an online utility that maps out where all the Raspberry Pi 3s are in the world. If you wanted to communicate with others and tell them where you Raspberry Pi 3 is, choose this option.To change the exact location of your Pi, change your user details or get rid of any information that you shared on Rastrack, go to www.rastrack.co.uk

### 9. Overclock

Overclocking is the act of tweaking the configurations in a way that is different to the manufacturer's standards to make it faster. When you select this option, a menu will appear telling you that overclocking could have an effect on your Raspberry Pi 3 lifespan. However, if you know what the right settings are, you can confidently change what you need to without affecting the lifetime of your Raspberry Pi 3.

Some of the presets may not be able to be changed as it will depend on configuration and power supply. If you can't use the overclock setting that you want to, hold the SHIFT key down to disable overclocking.

## 10. Advanced Option: Overscan

This setting lets you control how much border you see around the edge of the screen image and, if you have overspill on your particular monitor, to set the image to the right.

## 11. Advanced Option: Hostname

This lets you change the Raspberry Pi 3 name that will show up on other devices connected to the same network. Your Raspberry Pi 3 will have a default name of raspberrypi. Unless you have several Pi's attached to the network, you don't need to change this if you don't want to.

## 12. Advanced OptionL memory_split

The memory that is used by Raspberry Pi 3 is split between the CPU and the GPU, both of which run different programs. There are some programs that will want more GPU than CPU and vice versa so choosing this option will let you improve the performance of your Raspberry Pi 3 by giving the required processor the larger share of the performance.

## 13. Advanced Option: SSH

SSH allows you to create secure connections between computers and devices, usually so that you can set up controlling one device remotely from another. This setting allows you to enable or disable this option

## 14. Advanced Option: SPI

Raspberry Pi 3 communicates with other devices that are attached to the same board as add-ons through the SPI kernel module. This setting makes it easy to add sensors and other circuits to your board

## 15. Advanced Option: Audio

If you struggle to hear the audio from applications, this option forces the audio out of the HDMI or jack.

## 16. Advanced Option: Update

Use this for updating raspi-config whenever there is an update available. You do need to have an internet connection for this one.

When you are done, hit the Right arrow on your keyboard to go to the option Finish and then press Enter. You may need to restart your Raspberry Pi 3 but that will depend on what changes you have made.

To start up Raspi-config whenever you want to, go to the command prompt and type in the following command:

**sudo raspi-config**

## Important

If you are using the Jessie distribution, you might not be seeing raspi-config. The new release allows you to use a relegation of the tool which means that there is no longer any need to enter the above command. You can access Jessie configuration in the GUI by clicking on **Menu>Preferences>Raspberry Pi Configuration Tool.** The options are split into categories and are under 4 tabs and this is what you will find:

## System

- Boot options (to the desktop or to the command line interface)
- Auto login
- Overscan
- Expand Filesystem
- Change hostname
- Rastrack
- Change Password

## Interfaces

- SPI
- Serial
- SSH
- Camera
- I2C

## Performance

- GPU Memory
- Overclock

## Localization

- Set Time zone
- Set Locale
- Set Keyboard

Once you have made the changes the OS will want to restart so they can be put in place. Click on **Yes** and your device restarts

### Logging in for the First Time

When you switch on Raspberry Pi 3 you are asked to input your username and password. The default username is "pi" and the default password is "raspberry" both of which are case-sensitive. When you enter your password, you will not see any feedback on the screen like you are used to but this is for security reasons as it hides key activity. When you have typed in your password, hit the Enter key.

Once you have logged in and you have chosen to boot from CLI, the command line prompt will appear with the following line blinking on it:

**pi@raspberrypi ~ $**

You can now start to manage your Raspberry Pi 3 and all your programs and files.

Next, we are going to look at installing software on the Raspberry Pi 3.

# Chapter 4

# Installing Software on the Raspberry Pi 3

The Raspberry Pi is one of the best learning platforms in the world when compared to other similar boards. This is because of its flexibility and the compatibility of the operating system and, to implement gaming or computing projects, whether it be a media center to an Android emulation, you have to know how to install software that will run on the computer.

This could be anything from another operating system, some other software direct from Raspberry Pi store or from another repository. To be honest, installing software onto Raspberry Pi 3 is as easy as installing software on your smartphone, tablet or existing computer. However, if this is your first time on Linux, it may seem a little unfamiliar to begin with but you will easily learn how to do it. We talked in the last chapter how to install the operating system, Raspbian, onto your Raspberry Pi 3. Once you have done that, you can start installing software and the easiest way to begin is to use the command line.

Let's say that you wanted to install the Scrot tool. The command you would type in at the command line is:

## Sudo apt-get install scrot

The syntax, **apt-get install** is what we use to search all the repositories that are available for the software, to identify the right files and download them.

## Raspberry Pi Store

Linux is a unique product and it stands out from all the others and the developers have tried plenty of ways to make it easier to use. To that end, there have been distributions such as Mint and Ubuntu, both of which make it much easier for installing software onto Raspberry Pi 3.

First off, the package manager is similar to a search engine, filtering out results to get the right software or application. Most software repositories are available in specific distributions of Linux, just like a command line on a user interface that is mouse-driven.

Second, you can find software in app stores and Raspberry Pi has its own, called the Raspberry Pi Store. To download and install software from either place, you must first start a command line. Open the command prompt and type in:

**Sudo apt-get update && sudo apt-get install pistore**

As it does when you download software onto your computer, you will see a new icon on your desktop once the installation has finished. Double click on this icon to open it and you will see a window full of all the applications that are available for download. Just like the iOS app store or Google Play, the Pi store has lists of apps each with technical information and a few screenshots of each app.

Again, just like installing an application on a computer or mobile device, installing an app from the Raspberry Pi Store is very straightforward. Simply sing in or, if you haven't got one, create an account with the Store and start searching for what you want. Click on the Install button for an app and you chose from multiple payment methods. Once payment has been made successfully, the installation will begin. The only difference is because Pi is much smaller with less RAM, you can only install one app at a time. Some of the apps you can find on the Raspberry Pi Store include useful ones created specifically for Pi, such as LibreOffice, OpenTTD, and FreeCiv.

The hardest part about installing software on the Pi is learning the commands and where they need to be given for successful installations. Even though it can be something of a challenge, the Pi was actually created to teach people how to code and, in the next chapter, we will be looking at coding with Python.

There are also plenty of forums and websites where you can log on to get help and information, not just on Pi but on coding as well. You can also have the Raspberry Pi Store on your computer, making it easy to see if there are any updates to your applications

Generally, you will find that most of the user-generated software is either free or very cheap.

# Chapter 5

# Getting Started with Raspberry Pi 3 Programming

As with the software we talked about in the last chapter, you are not limited to one programming language with Raspberry Pi 3. Although Python is the primary languages, there are others that you can use. However, for this chapter, we are going to stick with Python because it is the one that is truly compatible with Linux.

Originally, Python was created as a teaching language, much like the Pi was developed as a teaching tool. Because of that, Python syntax is easy, very straightforward and uncomplicated. Because Python is also used across different operating systems, the number of instructions involved has reduced compare to other languages and it has since seen a huge surge in popularity for embedded systems and other apps.

To begin programming your Raspberry Pi 3 board you must first understand the basics of Python programming. If you are already familiar with these, skip this or use this chapter as a refresher. We are going to look briefly at the concepts of variables, loops, constants, decision making, basic operators, lists, modules, functions, and others that go into Python.

## Brief Overview of Python Programming

- Python is one of the easiest languages to learn and understand because it uses easy syntax and, unlike some languages, the code is compiled during runtime. Before a code is executed, any errors will be notified to you
- Python is an interactive language and can be used to develop a situation in which a question can be asked and the answers are them processed and will be prompted in the code output

- Python is for beginners and is the best one to start on if you are new to learning computer languages. It is used in a very large number of applications on the web and for the task of processing simple text

- Python is an objected-oriented language and all outputs are a real-time application. Python takes a lot of its concepts from C++.

Python is a cross-platform language and can be installed on the following:

- Windows CE
- Win 9x/NT/2000/XP/Vista/7/8/10
- OS/2
- DOS
- VMS/OpenVMS
- Psion
- VxWorks
- PalmOS
- UNIX systems (Solaris, Linux, FreeBSD, AIX, HP/UX, SunOS, IRIX, etc.)
- Acorn/RISC OS

- BeOS

- Macintosh (Intel, PPC, 68K)

- Amiga

- QNX

- Nokia mobile

- Java and .NET virtual machines

- Basic Syntax

There are two main types of programming:

- **Interactive Mode** – passing a command to invoke the interpreter to read and then respond to the instructions contained within the code. For example, if you were to type in the following:

Print ('Hello, Python!');

The output would be:

>> Hello, Python!

- **Script Mode** – attempting to invoke the interpreter by using a script parameter which starts to execute the entire script right to the end of the program. For example, allowing for the interpreter having the path that goes to the script with the file that is to be executed, and assuming that it is visible, we could do this:

$ python test.py
And the output:
Hello, Python!

## Python Concepts

- **Python Identifiers** – user-defined words that may be used as constants, variables, classes, functions or modules. An identifier may contain a to z, A to Z, 0 to 9 and (_) underscores. The use of any other special character will result in an error

- **Reserved Words** – Python contains several reserved keywords for use in specific functions and tasks and these cannot be used as identifiers. For example, "print" is reserved and cannot be used in as an identifier.

All keywords are lowercase only and these are the reserved keywords:

- and
- assert

- break
- class
- continue
- def
- del
- elif
- else
- except
- exec
- finally
- for
- from
- global
- if
- import
- in
- is
- lambda
- not
- or
- pass

- print
- raise
- return
- try
- while
- with
- yield

## Basic Python Operators

Operators are used to carry out basic logical and mathematical operations that are based on the input from the user and the output generated is for the logic. These are the Python operators:

- Arithmetic
- Logical
- Assignment
- Identity
- Comparison (Relational)
- Membership
- Bitwise

## Arithmetic:

Arithmetic operators perform basic arithmetic and are used where math calculation is required:

- Addition (+)
- Subtraction (-)
- Division (/)
- Multiplication (*)
- Modulus (%) – this gives the remainder after two terms have been divided
- Exponent (**)

## Logical:

Logical operators perform basic tasks, such as:

- AND – where two conditions are true, such A and B
- OR – where one of the conditions is true, such as A or B
- NOT – where the output is opposite of input

## Assignment:

Assignment operators are used for arithmetic or logical equations:

- = - assigns values to variables
- += - adds the operand on the right and assigns values to the operand on the left
- -= or *= - used the same as the above

**Identity**:

Identity operators are used to identify whether a statement is credible or not. It does this by assigning 'is' for statements where the operands on the left or the right point to the same object, in which case the output is 'true'. If not, the output is 'false'. "is not" operator is used to check both operands don't point to the same object, in which case, the output is 'true', if not, the output is 'false'

**Comparison**:

Comparison operators help to compare two quantities and the output is computed based on the observation:

- == - equal to
- != - not equal to
- >= - greater than or equal to

- <= - less than or equal to

## Bitwise:

Bitwise operators are used for several tasks that use numbers in binary form. For example:

A: 0 0 0 1 1 1 1 0

B: 1 1 0 0 0 0 1 1

_____

A&B: 0 0 0 0 0 0 1 0

A|B: 1 1 0 1 1 1 1 1

A^B: 1 1 0 1 1 1 0 1

~A: 1 1 1 0 0 0 0 1

## Membership:

Membership operators are used to test membership in sequences like strings, lists, tuples, etc.:

- in – checks the sequence and will evaluate 'true' if found, 'false' if not
- not in – checks for a specific character and evaluates 'true' if not found, 'false' if found

## Sample program:

This is a program that was written for the Raspberry Pi. It is to program the available GP10 pins on the Pi board and is assigned to a function:

```
#blink.py //opens the file containing the instructions

Import RPi.GPIO as GPIO //sets the default instructions to include GPIO port

Import time //Used to keep time
GPIO.setmode(GPIO.BOARD)
GPIO.setup(7, GPIO.OUT)
While true:
GPIO.output
(7, True)
Time.sleep(0.2)
GPIO.output(7, False)
Time.sleep (0.2)
```

This was written as a program to make the LED lights blink. In the main part of the program, GP10 pin number 7 is initialized. We start a while loop and as soon as the logic within "blink.py" is true, the loop will start to iterated until it becomes false. In the loop, if the logic for GP1o 7 is true, then the LED will be switched on for a period of 0.2 seconds and, if false, it will switch off for 0.2 seconds. This loop will be executed indefinitely until the RASPBERRY PI 3 has been switched off and the reason for this is, there is no false condition to stop the while loop.

**How to Fix Common Python Errors**

Although Python is user-friendly, it cans still be somewhat difficult if you are new to it and fluency will take some time to come. Let's look at a few common problems and how we fix them:

- **Confusing defaults and expressions for arguments that are function-based**

Python allows you to identify when function arguments are options by giving a default value. While this is a great feature, it can be confusing, especially when the default value stays mutable. The following is an example of a function definition in Python:

```
>>> def foo( bar=[ ] ) :                  # bar is an
option and defaults to [ ] if not specified
```

```
...bar.append ("baz")                    # this line
```
could be a problem, as you can see
```
...return bar
```

So, what is the error? You shouldn't think that an optional argument is going to automatically match the default expression whenever the function is used with no optional argument value. In this code, we could easily assume that, by calling foo(), we would automatically get a return of "baz" because, whenever foo() is used, the bar is set as []. The next example shows you what would happen when you do this:

```
>>> foo ( )
[ "baz" ]
>>> foo ( )
[ "baz" , "baz" ]
>>> foo ( )
[ "baz" , "baz" , "baz" ]
```

Notice that the default value, "baz" keeps changing to an existing list each time foo() is used rather than making a brand-new list. When you get into advanced programming, you will find that a default value that is associated with any function argument will be calculated just once and that one time is when the function will be defined. What that means is, the bar argument will be initialized to its default but foo() must be defined first and that will result in any more foo() calls being used in the exact same list in which bar was first initialized.

This example shows how to fix this:

```
>>> def foo (bar=None ) :
... if bar is None;
...  bar = [ ]
... bar.append( "baz" )
... return bar
...
>>> foo ( )
[ "baz" ]
>>> foo ( )
[ "baz" ]
>>> foo ( )
[ "baz" ]
```

**Not using class variables the right way**

```
>>> class A(object) :
... X = 1
```

. . .

>>> class B(A) :

. . . pass

. . .

>>> class C(A) :

. . . pass

. . .

>>> print A.x, B.x, C.x

1 1 1

This makes sense as a launch point but let's go a little further:

>>> B.x = 2

>>>print A.x, B.x, C.x

1 2 1

This one also makes sense and is also correct

>>> A.x = 3

>>> print A.x, B.x, C.x

3 2 3

Whoa! Hold on a minute; A.x was the only one meant to change so what happened with C.x? In the Python language, a variable is handled as a dictionary internally and will abide by the MRO Method

Resolution Order. In the sample code, attribute x is not in class C; instead, only the base classes will look it up and in this example, that is A. What this means is that C doesn't have an x property of its own, separate form A s, when we reference C.x, it is sent to A.x.

**Make sure you use the right parameters**

```
>>> try :
...             1 = [ "a" , "b" }
...             int (1[2])
...             except ValueError, IndexError:        #
To catch both exceptions, right
...             pass
...
```

Traceback            (most recent call last) :
File "<stdin>" , line 3, in <module>
IndexError : list index out of range

What went wrong here is that there is no list of properly specified exceptions in the except statement. In except Exception, e is supposed to connect the exception with what has been made as the second specified parameter. In the example, e is the second parameter, making it available for inspection if needed. The result of this is an IndexError exception that has not been used properly by the except statement; instead it is bound to a parameter that is called IndexError

The right way to use multiple exceptions in an except statement is to make sure the parameter is specified as a tuple, containing all exceptions that are to be caught. As well, it is also a good idea to use the keyword "as" because that is a more universal syntax.

```
>>> try:
...           1 = ["a , "b"]
...           int (1[2])
...           except (ValueError, IndexError) as e:
...           pass
...
>>>
```

## Mistaking the Python scope rules

Python Scope is based on the LEGB rule – Local, Enclosing, Global, Built-in. To those of you used to

Python, this is probably straightforward but there are lots of things here that can cause errors. Look at this piece of common Python code that can cause a problem:

```
>>> x = 10
>>> def foo():
...     x += 1
...     print x
...
>>> foo()
Traceback (most recent call last):
  File "<stdin>", line 1, in <module>
  File "<stdin>", line 2, in foo
UnboundLocalError: local variable 'x' referenced before assignment
```

The error happens because when you make an assignment to a variable inside a scope, Python will automatically assume that the assignment is local to the scope and it will then shadow any other variable of the same name. It might come as a bit of a surprise when you see then UnboundLocalError in a piece of code that worked previously just because you added an assigned statement into the function body. It can also happen when you use a list as well:

```
>>> lst = [1, 2, 3]
>>> def foo1():
...    lst.append(5)  # This works ok...
...
>>> foo1()
>>> lst
[1, 2, 3, 5]

>>> lst = [1, 2, 3]
>>> def foo2():
...    lst += [5]    # ... but this bombs!
...
>>> foo2()
Traceback (most recent call last):
  File "<stdin>", line 1, in <module>
  File "<stdin>", line 2, in foo
UnboundLocalError: local variable 'lst' referenced before assignment
```

This will allow foo1 to run as it should do but fo2 will not. The reason for this is exactly the same as in the previous example. In this case, foo1 isn't connected to an assignment to 1st but foo2 is. What you need to remember is that 1sr+=[f5] is the same as lst=lst+[5] – what this is doing is attempting to assign the value to 1st but the value is based on 1st and Python will assume this to be local scope – it hasn't actually been defined.

**Changing a list and iterating over it**:
```
>>> odd = lambda x : bool(x % 2)
>>> numbers = [n for n in range(10)]
>>> for i in range(len(numbers)):
...    if odd(numbers[i]):
...        del numbers[i]  # BAD: Deleting item from a
list while iterating over it
...
Traceback (most recent call last):
        File "<stdin>", line 2, in <module>
IndexError: list index out of range
```

If you are experienced at programming, you will know that, when you delete any item form a list or an array while you are iterating over it, you will get a problem. The above example shows a very blatant mistake but you won't always see it so easily and even advanced developers still get tripped up by this.

Python uses a lot of different paradigms that streamline and simplify the code. One of the benefits of using simple code is that there is less chance of mistakes happening. One paradigm is called the List Comprehension paradigm, useful for avoiding the issue in the above code. Here's how it works:

```
>>> odd = lambda x : bool(x % 2)
>>> numbers = [n for n in range(10)]
>>> numbers[:] = [n for n in numbers if not odd(n)]
# ahh, the beauty of it all
>>> numbers
[0, 2, 4, 6, 8]
```

**Not properly understanding how Python binds closures**:

```
>>> def create_multipliers():
...     return [lambda x : i * x for i in range(5)]
>>> for multiplier in create_multipliers():
```

```
...     print multiplier(2)
...
```

You would expect to see this output:

0

2

4

6

8

But this is very different from what you would actually see:

8

8

8

8

8

The reason this happens is because of Python's late binding behavior. The variable values in closures are looked up at the time the inner function is called. Every time the returned functions are called, a value of i is found within the surrounding scope. There are those who think the only solution is a hack but it isn't. This is the solution:

```
>>> def create_multipliers():
...     return [lambda x, i=i : i * x for i in range(5)]
...
>>> for multiplier in create_multipliers():
...     print multiplier(2)
...
0
2
4
6
8
```

The solution is to use default arguments that will create an anonymous function that goes in your favor. Some don't agree with this but you should understand how it works.

## Circular module dependencies

Let's assume that we have two files called a.py and b.py. Both files will import the other file:

In a.py :

```
import b
def f():
```

```
    return b.x
print f()
In b.py:
import a
x = 1
def g():
    print a.f()
First attempt to import a.py:
>>> import a
1
```

As you can see, that works just fine, we have a proper circular import. These import types are not too much of an issue because Python is well aware that it shouldn't try to import the same thing twice. It does, however, depend on the point that the module is trying to access the functions or variables that are defined and that's where problems can arise. In the example, a.py had no trouble importing b.py because the latter didn't need to get anything from a.py at the time it was being imported. However, the only reference we have to b.py to a can be found in a.f()

but the ca is to g() – there just isn't any reason for a or b.py to invoke g().

This example shows what would happen if you attempted to import b.py:

```
>>> import b
Traceback (most recent call last):
        File "<stdin>", line 1, in <module>
        File "b.py", line 1, in <module>
    import a
        File "a.py", line 6, in <module>
        print f()
        File "a.py", line 4, in f
        return b.x
```

AttributeError: 'module' object has no attribute 'x'

This just can't work because, at the same time as you import b.py, Python is also trying to import a.py, calling f(), and this then attempts to access b.x. This has not yet been defined properly. The best solution is to make b.py import a.py in g():

```
x = 1
```

```
def g():
    import a           # This is evaluated only when g() is
called
    print a.f()
```

This time, everything works as it should:

```
>>> import b
>>> b.g()
1           # Printed a first time since module 'a' calls
'print f()' at the end
1           # Printed a second time, this one is our call
to 'g'
```

## Name clashing with library modules

One of the great things about Python is the number of library modules it comes with but, if you are not an experienced coder or if you are not on the lookout for it, you can easily get into trouble with name clashes between a module in the library and one of your own. This can kick up some very complicated issues because Python will then try to import a separate library and this will lead to it attempting to import the standard Python version. The system won't know which one it should import so the only solution is to take care when you are choosing your names.

## Python 2 and Python 3

Some people use Python 2 while others use Python 3 and not understanding the difference between them can cause problems. Have a look at this example:

```python
import sys
def bar(i):
    if i == 1:
        raise KeyError(1)
    if i == 2:
        raise ValueError(2)
def bad():
    e = None
    try:
        bar(int(sys.argv[1]))
    except KeyError as e:
        print('key error')
    except ValueError as e:
        print('value error')
    print(e)
```

bad()

In Python 2, this will run properly:

```
$ python foo.py 1
key error

1
$ python foo.py 2
value error

2
```

Whereas, if you attempt to run it in Python 3, this will happen:

```
$ python3 foo.py 1
key error
Traceback (most recent call last):
  File "foo.py", line 19, in <module>
    bad()
  File "foo.py", line 17, in bad
    print(e)
```

UnboundLocalError: local variable 'e' referenced before assignment

Clearly, this piece of code will not work in Python 3 and he reason for that is, in 3, we can access the exception object outside the scope of the except block. To avoid this happening, ensure that you refer to the exception object outside of the scope so it can still be accessed. If we apply that to the previous example, that can now be accessed in both 2 and 3:

```
import sys
def bar(i):
    if i == 1:
        raise KeyError(1)
    if i == 2:
        raise ValueError(2)
def good():
    exception = None
    try:
        bar(int(sys.argv[1]))
    except KeyError as e:
        exception = e
        print('key error')
    except ValueError as e:
        exception = e
        print('value error')
    print(exception)
good()
```

## Not using the _del_ method the right way

Let's assume that we have the following example in a file called mod.py:

```
import foo
class Bar(object):
        ...
  def __del__(self):
     foo.cleanup(self.myhandle)
```

Next, let's assume that you tried to do this from another file called_mod.py:

```
import mod
mybar = mod.Bar()
```

This will throw up an AttributeError exception because all the global variables are set at None when the interpreter closes. When you use _del_, foo is already set at None. The solution to this is in using atexit.register() because, when you program has completed execution, all registered handlers will be thrown of before the interpreter closes. The solution should look like this example:

```
import foo
```

```
import atexit
def cleanup(handle):
    foo.cleanup(handle)
class Bar(object):
    def __init__(self):
        ...
        atexit.register(cleanup, self.myhandle)
```

By adding in atexit.register, you are providing a clean
and reliable way of using whatever cleanup function
is needed for normal termination of the program. It
would be up to foo.cleanup to decide what should be
done with the self.myHandle object so make sure you
have set it up properly.

You will need to get a better understanding of Python
programming but, when you first start to use your
Raspberry Pi 3, you will come up against errors –
some will be easy to fix, others won't. Sometimes you
will see straightaway what the error is while other
times you won't see the problem for looking. There is
always a solution to any error and you will find it in
this book or in the internet.

Next, we are going to look at a few projects you can do with your Raspberry Pi 3.

# Chapter 6

# Project Ideas

Now you know more about your Raspberry Pi 3, it's time to start looking at some projects, things you can do with your Raspberry Pi 3 board. Here, we have three different projects with full instructions on how to make them.

**Raspberry Pi XBMC**

XBMC is the popular media streaming center and getting it running on your Raspberry Pi 3 is simple. You do need to get the right materials, though, so here's a list:

- Raspberry Pi 3
- HDMI video cable (you can use composite if you prefer)
- Minimum 8 GB Class 10 MicroSD card

- Card reader (external if you don't have a built-in one)
- USB mouse and keyboard
- Ethernet cable
- Micro USB power supply – 5V 2A is best
- Remote control if you don't want to use the keyboard and mouse to control the media center
- USB Hard drive – this is optional and is for storing videos if you don't want to stream them from another computer
- Raspberry Pi case – again, optional, this is only to protect the Raspberry Pi 3 board
- 3.5mm stereo audio cable – optional – only required if you use analog video and want external speakers or to use the internal speakers on your TV. If you use HDMI, you don't need one of these
- Raspbmc Installer – this will put the properly optimized Raspberry Pi XBMC onto the SD card, or you can use OSMC

## What to Expect

While XBMC is a powerful media center and the Raspberry Pi 3 makes a great choice for one, there are some things that it just won't do. For starters, don't expect it to stream content that comes from the internet and it may not be perfect at 1080p video – you might have to settle for 720p. Much of that will depend on where the audio is being played from – streaming from a USB hard drive is much smoother than over the network.

You might also find that the menus are somewhat slower than you expect and you might not get such great skins on it either. That said, it is a great way of building a secondary media center that works well for 720p playback so let's get started building it.

## Step 1 - Install Raspbmc to your SD card.

This is absolutely the first step before you start hooking everything up and here's how to do it on Windows:

- Insert the MicroSD into your PC

- Download the installer and run it on the desktop
- Download it to your SD card and then safely eject the card

## Step 2 – Get Raspberry Pi 3 hooked up and install Raspbmc

The next step is to connect Raspberry Pi 3 t the TV so plug the HDMI into the TV, connect the Ethernet cable to your router, pop the SD card in and plug in the power cable. Plug it into a power source and you should see the Raspberry Pi 3 switch on and boot from the card – the installation will start.

At this stage, you don't need to do anything else. Make sure everything is installing and then leave it for about 15 to 25 minutes. When it has finished, it will boot to XBMC.

## Step 3 – Tweak the Settings

You are almost done! All you need to do now is tweak some settings so that everything runs as it should so here's what is recommended:

- **Resolution** - go to **Settings>System>Video Output.** If you only want to watch 720p, change it to 720p. This will make everything just a little snappier.

- **Overscan** – go to **Settings>System>Video Output>Video Calibration.** Calibrate to make the picture fit the screen using the wizard

- **System Performance Profile** – go to **Programs>Raspbmc Settings>System Configuration.** This is specific to Pi that lets you overclock and have everything going a little faster and smoother. Try the "Fast" setting to speed things up without losing stability. "Super" will run even faster but you may get some instability issues

- **MPEG2 Codec License** – You must purchase this from the Raspberry Pi Store and then set it up under **Programs>Raspbmc Settings>System Configuration.** It will let you play MPEG 2 videos which can't be played on the Pi out of the box. If you don't have any of these videos, forget this step.

Your XBMC media center is set up so enjoy!

## A VPN Server

You don't need any special equipment to turn your Raspberry Pi 3 into a VPN and Web Proxy server. We are going to be using LogMeInHamachi to create the VPN so what you will need is:

- A free account at LogMeIn. Hamachi will automatically create the VPN for you so need to be messing about with port forwarding, static IP addresses or trying to get around firewalls.
- Privoxy – this app is to be paired with Hamachi so that secure web browsing can be enabled, be it from within or external to the network. I'll talk you through downloading it in a while
- Raspberry Pi 3
- HDMI or composite video cable
- Minimum 8GB Class 10 MicroSD card
- Card reader
- USB mouse and keyboard
- Ethernet cable
- Micros USB power supply

# Step 1 – Connect and Configure Raspberry Pi 3

You should already have Raspbian on your RASPBERRY PI 3 if you have followed the instructions in this book. If not, go back and install it now and then change the default keyboard if you are not using your Raspberry Pi 3 from the UK. Some commands are going to need special characters which are changed to different places in the UK keyboard. If you already have Raspbian set up, go to the command prompt and type in:

sudo dpkg-reconfigure keyboard-configuration

Now follow the on-screen prompts to change the keyboard to your country and then restart by typing in the sudo reboot command or, at the prompt type in the following:

invoke-rc.d keyboard-setup start

# Step 2 – Update and Then Install Hamachi

You will need a couple of extra packages for Hamachi and they may not be available in your Raspbian image so, first, we need to update them. Don't skip this step because it can save you a lot of hassle later down the line. First, update by typing:

sudo apt-get update

Now type in the following to install LSB:

sudo apt-get install —fix-missing lsb lsb-core

Wait while it updates and then you can download Hamachi for Linux. Type this in:

sudo wget https://secure.logmein.com/labs/logmein-hamachi_2.1.0.86-1_armel.deb

Now type the following command in to install Hamachi:

sudo dpkg -1 logmein-hamachi_2.1.0.86-1_armel.deb

**Step 3 – Configure Hamachi**

On your Raspberry Pi 3, run this command to connect it to the LogMeIn account and to create a new network with Hamachi:

sudo hamachi login

sudo hamachi attach [type in your logmein.com email]

sudo hamachi set-nick [type in a nickname for your Raspberry Pi 3]

On another computer, go to LogMeIn and sign in. Under Networks, click on My Networks and you will see your Raspberry Pi 3 is attempting to connects and make a new network. Give it permission and make a note of the network ID – it will be 9 digits.

Now go back to Raspberry Pi 3 and input this command:

sudo hamachi do-join [type in the network ID you made a note of]

Type your LogMeIn password in and, if necessary, go to the other computer and approve the join request. Now the Raspberry Pi 3 is part of the new Hamachi VPN. Go back to LogMeIn on your computer and write down the virtual IP address that has been assigned to your Pi – you will need it in a bit

Now start the SSH server so that you can remotely control Raspberry Pi 3 by typing in this command:

sudo /etc/init.d/ssh start

## Step 4 – Install Hamachi to your PC

Almost there – go to the <u>Hamachi download</u> page and download the Hamachi client for your computer OS. Once you have done that, click on **Network>Join** and then SSH into your Raspberry Pi 3 or access your network files. You will want something like PuTTY in Windows or Terminal in Mac or Linux systems to SSH into the RASPBERRY PI 3 address.

## Step 5 – Optional – Install Privoxy

You can use your Raspberry Pi 3 as a proxy server and you do this by connecting Hamachi and Privoxy. This will enable your web browsing sessions to be secured and encrypted when you use public wi-fi. Here's how to set Privoxy up on your Raspberry Pi 3:

- Install Privoxy by executing this command:

sudo apt-get install privoxy

- Use this command to start Privoxy:

etc/init.d/privoxy start

- Input this to open the config file in your text editor:

sudo nano /etc/privoxy/config

- Look for the following code line

listen-address localhost:8118

- Add a # to the beginning of the line to comment it out
- Now add a new line underneath it:

listen-address [the IP address assigned to your Pi by Hamachi]:8118 (e.g., 25.1.1.1:8118)

- Press CTRL+X to save the file and restart Privoxy with this command:

sudo service privoxy restart

All you need to do now is set your proxy server as Privoxy on your other computer/s. To do that:

- **Google Chrome** – Settings>Show Advanced Settings>Network>Change Proxy Settings
- **Firefox** – Preferences>Advanced>Network>Configure How Firefox Connects to the Internet>Settings

Type the Raspberry Pi 3 IP address in (the one assigned by Hamachi) where the proxy address is and input the port as 8118.

**An Airplay Receiver**

Turning your Raspberry Pi 3 into an Airplay receiver is dead simple but you will need to pick up a few materials first. You will need:

- Raspberry Pi 3
- HDMI cable, or composite if you prefer
- Minimum 8 GB micro SD card, class 10 or better
- Card reader
- USB mouse and keyboard
- Micro USB power supply, minimum 700mA at 5V
- 3.5 mm stereo audio cable
- Wi-Fi USB adapter – so you can send the music from your iPad or iPhone to your Raspberry Pi 3.
- USB Sound Card – to beef up the sound from your Raspberry Pi 3 as it isn't that great.

- A sterol with speakers that allow for audio input
- iPhone, iPad or iPod Touch or a computer that has iTunes installed as a music source. You could also try an Android device that has DoubleTwist installed on it

## What to Expect

Raspberry Pi 3 is ideal for turning into an Airplay device and, when you are done building this, you will have a neat box that connects to your stereo and has functions that are somewhat like speakers with Airplay enabled. When you plug in and boot up, everything that is required to start Airplay will automatically load so you don't need an external keyboard or monitor. In essence, you can stream your music to any speaker for a fraction of the cost of an Airport Express and you can still use your Raspberry Pi 3 for any other project. What you won't get is Airplay Mirroring so you can't send videos.

## Step 1 – Connect and Configure Your Raspberry Pi 3

The Airplay function works well with Raspbian which you should already have installed n your Raspberry Pi 3. If you are looking to have the Airplay receiver automatically start without using a monitor or keyboard, you must set up Raspbian so it automatically logs you in. When you are setting up Raspbian through raspi-config, look for the setting "Start Desktop on Boot" and set it to Yes. If you already have Raspbian set up, go to the command prompt and type in the following:

sudo raspi-config

Now we must add a few packages that you may not be in your image so, type these commands in and execute each one:

sudo apt-get update

sudo apt-get upgrade

It might take a while to do the update so leave things be for a while and be patient. Once your Raspberry Pi 3 has rebooted back to Raspbian and all is working as it should do, we can start setting up the Airplay functions. You can use console commands to set everything up but we are going to use the interface on Raspbian as it somewhat easier.

## Step 2 Setting Up

- **Set Up the USB Wi-Fi Adapter**

The first step is to make sure your Wi-Fi adapter is working and with Raspbian that is dead easy:

- If you haven't already done so, connect your Wi-Fi adapter to your Raspberry Pi 3
- On the desktop, open the Wi-Fi configuration application
- Choose your specific adapter form the drop-down menu
- Sign into your network

That is all you need to do for the Wi-Fi adapter. If you want, go to the desktop and open the Midori browser just to check that he internet works. Raspbian will remember your choices so, even if the adapter is disconnected at any time, as soon as it is reconnected, it will load up automatically.

- **Set Up Your Sound Card**

Connect your sound card to the Raspberry Pi 3 with the USB connection and then use the 3.5 mm audio cable to connect it to your chosen stereo. We need to use a terminal command so open LXTerminal from the desktop and type this in:

aplay -l

You should see something along the lines of "Card 1: set [name of device], devices 0: USB Audio" displayed by the card. This means that Raspberry Pi 3 has recognized it so we can test the sound. To do that, type in:

Alsamixer

The software need to test the audio output will now load up. Press the F6 key to change the type of output and choose your sound card. To test the output, type in:

speaker-test

If all is well, a sound should come from your speakers to confirm that the sound card is working.

Lastly, Raspbian will not load the card automatically when it boots up like it does with the Wi-Fi adapter. We need to make a few small changes to the configuration file so type in the this:

cd /etc/modprobe.d

sudo nano alsa-base.conf

The specified file (alsa-base.conf) will now open. Go down to near the end and look for the line that says:

options snd-usb-audio index=-2

Add a # to the beginning of the lien to comment it out and then press Ctrl+X to save the edits and come out.

Now, every time you reboot your Raspberry Pi 3, both the Wi-Fi adapter and the sound card will automatically work.

- **Install Shairport Airplay Emulator**

This is the software needed to make Airplay work and it is going to take a while to set it up. It isn't hard but do allow about half an hour to do this because there is quite a bit of software to download and install.

First, there are some things to install before we even get to Shairport so, in your console, type this in:

sudo apt-get install git libao-dev libssl-dev libcrypt-openssl-rsa-perl libio-socket-inet6-perl libwww-perl avahi-utils libmodule-build-perl

Now be patient and leave this running for a bit. When it has finished, there is an update to install so input this:

git clone https://github.com/njh/perl-net-sdp.git
perl-net-sdp
cd perl-net-sdp
perl Build.PL
sudo ./Build
sudo ./Build test
sudo ./Build install
cd ..

When the module has been installed, and it will take a while, we can finally go to Shairport. At the prompt, get back to your home directory and then type in:

git clone
https://github.com/hendrikw82/shairport.git
cd shairport
make

Now we can run Shairport by typing this in:

/shairport.pl -a AirPi

This command is used to start Shairport with your Raspberry Pi 3 called "AirPi" – change it to whatever suits you. On your iPhone, iPad or iPod Touch, choose your music app and tap on the button that says Airplay. You should now see your Raspberry Pi 3 listed as one of the output devices. Tap on it and you should hear music streaming from your USB sound card within seconds

Not quite done yet, though. When you start your Raspberry Pi 3, Shairport won't automatically start so, because we need it to work without any peripherals, there is one more thing to do. Go to your home directory at the prompt and type in:

cd shairport
make install
cp shairport.init.sample /etc/init.d/shairport

```
cd /etc/init.d
chmod a+x shairport
update-rc.d shairport defaults
```

Lastly, Shairport must be added as a launch item so type in:

```
sudo nano shairport
```

This will load the Shairport file that we have to make some edits to. Search the file for a line with DAEMON_ARGS in it and change it so it reads like this:

```
DAEMON_ARGS="-w $PIDFILE -a AirPi"
```

Pres Ctrl+X to save the edit and come out and you are now all set up. Shairport will launch every time you start up your Raspberry Pi 3 and you can take it wherever you want. Provided the sound card and the USB Wi-Fi adapter are connected, they will load up with Shairport whenever your Raspberry Pi 3 is rebooted or turned on. You won't need to add a keyboard, mouse or monitor for it all to work.

To use the Airplay function now, all you need to do is connect the Raspberry Pi 3 to a power source and let it boot up. It should take about 30 to 40 seconds for the Raspbian OS to load and then you can easily and instantly stream all your music through your Raspberry Pi 3.

# Chapter 7

# Hints and Tips

While some of these will be common sense to those who are experienced at Linux, you might just learn something you didn't know. These tips will help to make your use of your Raspberry Pi 3:

- **Completing Command lines**

There is no need to type out long filenames, paths, and commands. Simply type in the first few characters and press the Tab button. If bash or shell (the command line interpreters) can work out what you are typing in, it will auto-fill the rest. If not, press Tab again and you will get a list of the possible to choose from.

- **Command History**

Bash will keep a history of all the commands you type in. When you are at the command prompt, click the

UP key to go through all your recently types commands – keep clicking until you get to the one you want. When you find it, press Enter to execute it.

- **Going Straight to the Start or End of a Command**

If you want to go to the start or to the end of a command, perhaps to correct a mistake, click on Ctrl+A for the start and Ctrl+E for the end.

- **Use Alt+F1 to F6 Keys to Switch Screens**

Provided you are not in the GUI environment, you can multitask. Press ALT and F1 through to F6 keys to switch between your terminal screens

- **sudo !!**

When you type out a whole command and then get told that, to execute it, you have to be a superuser, can be incredibly irritating. Type in sudo !! (sudo bang bang) and the previous command will be executed as root.

- **Screenshots**

First, install scrot (type in sudo apt-get install scrot at the command prompt) and you will be able to take screenshots in the GUI. Once installed, execute scrot in the terminal window so that you can save a png of your desktop into your working directory. Scrot can also be configured. At the prompt, type in scrot-h and all the configuration options that are available.

- **Log in Remotely**

If you wanted to access the command line on your Raspberry Pi 3 from another computer, you would type in sudo raspi-config and then select the option for enabling SSH. Then, you would type in ifconfig to get access to the IP on your Raspberry Pi 3. If you use Mac or Linux, type in ssh pi@[ip address] or, on Windows, you can use PuTTY.

- **One Line Python Web Server**

If you wanted to create a web server using just a single command, you would type in python -m SimpleHTTPServer and execute it. All the files that are in the working directory can then be accessed through the IP address of your Raspberry Pi 3. If you want to serve that particular page, add in an index.html file. If not, you will see a file directory

- **raspberrypi.local**

If you struggle to remember your Raspberry Pi 3 IP address when you need to get to it through the network, you can install avahi. Simply type in sudo apt-get install avahi-daemon at the command prompt and execute it. Now you can use raspberrypi.local instead of the actual IP address.

# Conclusion

Thank you for downloading this book!

I hope that you now have a better understanding of how to use your Raspberry Pi 3 and how to use it to build some neat little projects. I also hope that you have now developed a passion for coding and how to use it to do pretty much what you want. Coding in itself is a fun thing to do but, paired with a neat computer like the Raspberry Pi 3, the world truly is your oyster and you have a lot of fun ahead of you – as well as a lot of learning

The next step is to continue learning. Keep your eye open for updates because, as with everything in computing and coding, nothing stays the same. All I can do here is give you a basic start but there is plenty more to learn and plenty more projects out there for you to get your teeth into. There are constant updates, both the Raspberry Pi and, in particular, to Python computer programming language. Join forums and online clubs, get all the advice you can and keep up to date with all the changes in the world of Raspberry Pi programming.

Also, keep in mind that the Raspberry Pi is designed for people who want to learn to code, want to learn how to make new things, people like you. So, get inventing and see what you can create with your Raspberry Pi 3. Start with the three projects in this book and then build on them. Create robots, computers, phones and media centers. Make a Lego car, a retro arcade gaming machine and all sorts of other neat things, whether they are useful or just for a bit of fun!

Finally, I'd like to ask you a favor. If you enjoyed this book, if you found it helpful, please post a review for me on Amazon. I would greatly appreciate it and it helps other buyers as well.

Thank you and good luck!

Printed in Poland
by Amazon Fulfillment
Poland Sp. z o.o., Wrocław